THE WORLD C

THE WII
in the
WILLOWS

Antoinnette Rawlings

*T*he *Wind in the Willows* by Kenneth Grahame has enchanted readers since its publication in 1908. Widely regarded as one of the great classics of children's literature, the book follows the exploits of four animal friends who live in the English countryside. The endearing escapades of Ratty, Mole, Badger and Toad combine adventure and camaraderie with aspects of morality, and tell of the social struggle between the river-bankers and the wild-wooders.

Evoking the rivers, woodlands and byways of an idyllic pastoral landscape, the setting is much inspired by the author's own childhood, largely spent with his grandmother in Berkshire and at school in Oxford. Throughout his life, tainted by tragedy and disappointment, Kenneth Grahame's happiest times were when he explored the countryside and was close to nature.

Although considered a master of English prose, and already a respected author before the emergence of *The Wind in the Willows*, Kenneth Grahame only wrote in his spare time and never intended the tales about Toad and his friends to be published. The characters had first appeared in bedtime stories made up for his son, Alastair, and the version as we know it evolved through a series of letters written to him.

Grahame wrote very little after its publication, but the charm and appeal to children and adults alike has endured, and *The Wind in the Willows* remains one of the most popular children's books of all time.

Important Dates

1859   Kenneth Grahame born in Edinburgh on 8 March, the third child of James Cunningham Grahame and Bessie Grahame (née Ingles).

1866   The children are summoned back to Scotland by their father but he abandons them for good shortly afterwards.

1878   Kenneth's dream of going to Oxford University is shattered through lack of family finance and support. A family connection leads to a career at the Bank of England.

1893   *Pagan Papers* published.

1898   *Dream Days* published.

1900   The Grahames' only child, Alastair (known as 'Mouse') is born; he is thought to have partly inspired the creation of Mr Toad.

1904   Kenneth begins to tell Alastair bedtime stories from which the main characters for *The Wind in the Willows* evolve.

1907   Kenneth starts to write a series of letters to Alastair from Cornwall and London, which outline Toad's adventures.

1910   The Grahames find their dream house – Boham's Farmhouse, at Blewbury, near Didcot, Oxfordshire – and become increasingly reclusive.

1924   The Grahames return to England and move to Church Cottage, Pangbourne, Berkshire.

1929   *Toad of Toad Hall*, a play by A.A. Milne, published and performed.

1931   The 38th edition of *The Wind in the Willows* published with E.H. Shepard's black and white illustrations.

1951   The 100th edition of *The Wind in the Willows* published in Britain, illustrated by Arthur Rackham.

1864   Mrs Grahame dies of scarlet fever. The children go to live with their maternal grandmother at The Mount, Cookham Dean in Berkshire.

1868   Kenneth and his brother Willie are sent to St Edward's School, Oxford; Kenneth is an outstanding pupil, despite the trauma of Willie dying three years later.

1892   By now, Kenneth is writing in his spare time, and has become a regular contributor to *St James Gazette* and the *National Observer*.

1895   *The Golden Age* published; it becomes a classic of its day.

1899   Kenneth Grahame marries Elspeth Thomson.

1903   Kenneth Grahame is shot at during an attack at the Bank of England.

1906   The Grahame family leaves London and settles in Cookham Dean.

1908   In June, Kenneth Grahame takes early retirement from the Bank of England. In October, *The Wind in the Willows* is published by Methuen & Co.

1920   Alastair is found dead on train tracks in Oxford. Kenneth and Elspeth embark on an extended trip to Italy.

1926   Kenneth turns down an invitation by his literary agent, Curtis Brown, to write his autobiography, but does note down some early recollections, which he calls *Oxford Through a Boy's Eyes*.

1930   E.H. Shepard visits Kenneth at Pangbourne to discuss illustrating a new edition of *The Wind in the Willows*.

1932   Kenneth Grahame dies at his home in Pangbourne on 6 July.

1969   E.H. Shepard produces full-colour illustrations for *The Wind in the Willows*.

Kenneth Grahame's Childhood

Kenneth Grahame was born on 8 March 1859 at 32 Castle Street, Edinburgh, to Bessie (née Ingles) and James Cunningham Grahame, an Edinburgh lawyer whose family was descended from Robert the Bruce. Queen Victoria's physician attended the birth and the baby arrived into a happy, upper-middle class Scottish family. Cunningham Grahame was later appointed Sherriff-Substitute of Argyllshire at Inverary, but tragedy was to change the family's prospects. In 1864, Bessie died of scarlet fever shortly after giving birth to her fourth child. Her last words were, 'It's all been so lovely.'

Kenneth also became seriously ill, whilst his father turned to alcohol to escape his grief. It was decided that the children should go into the care of Bessie's mother, Mary, known as Granny Ingles. Cunningham's brother, John, would meet any financial needs.

Granny Ingles' home – The Mount, Cookham Dean, Berkshire – was a rambling old house surrounded by several acres of land, near the River Thames and Quarry Wood. Here a small boy could explore magical gardens and orchards and create

> Of being sent to school, Kenneth later wrote that he was 'a small school-boy kicked out of his nest into the draughty, uncomfortable outer world'.

a world of make-believe. This experience, which combined a child's wonderment at the natural world around him, together with a yearning for lost family, influenced most of Kenneth's adult writing.

The Mount was home for only two years; in 1865 a heavy gale caused the chimney to fall in and the following spring the family moved to Fernhill Cottage, Cranbourne, near Windsor Great Park. That same year, Cunningham attempted to bring his family together again in Scotland. However, unable to cope, he left for France in 1867, and was not heard from again.

Sent to St Edward's School, Oxford, in 1868, Kenneth was clearly gifted. He won classics prizes, wrote for and edited the school *Chronicle* and became Head of School, despite the trauma of his elder brother, Willie, dying from pneumonia in 1871 aged 16.

Kenneth longed to go to Oxford University but Uncle John refused to provide the financial support. It was a bitter disappointment. Instead, a family connection led to the promise of a place at the Bank of England. In the interim, Kenneth worked in his uncle's London firm of Parliamentary Agents: Grahame, Currie and Spens.

▲ St Edward's School, Oxford.

A Career in Banking

Kenneth Grahame was accepted as a junior clerk at the Bank of England on 12 December 1878. Placed first in the Election of Candidates (the entrance examination) for that year, his total score of 518 out of 640 remains one of the highest ever attained.

Despite his misgivings, Kenneth was very good at his job. He rose through the ranks and was appointed Secretary on 6 October 1898 at the age of 39, and remains one of the youngest on record to hold that office. As the Governor's right-hand man, the post was highly responsible. Kenneth oversaw a large department, which ensured that the decisions of the governing body – the Court of Directors – were implemented, managed the legal side of operations and looked after the buildings. On a daily basis, Kenneth would have seen the Bank's garden – a small haven of nature in the middle of the City, complete with water fountain.

On 15 June 1908, Kenneth Grahame wrote a letter of resignation citing ill health and strain. However, a former colleague, W. M. Acres, states in a letter that Kenneth's abrupt departure was due to the bullying attitude of one of the Bank's Directors, Walter Cunliffe, who later became Governor. A dispute had led Kenneth to say that

▲ The Bank of England, Threadneedle Street, London, *c.* 1890.

➤ Interior of the Bank of England, as Kenneth Grahame would have known it.

Cunliffe was 'no gentleman', and according to Acres: 'The retirement was very sudden, as I believe Mr Grahame did not appear at the Bank again after the day the incident happened.' Kenneth was entitled to an annual pension of £791 but was only awarded £400, which might reflect the consequences of disagreeing with a Director.

➤ Illustration from *The Daily Graphic*, captioned 'The shooting outrage at the Bank of England: the officials overpowering the assailant with the fire hose'.

THE SHOOTING INCIDENT

On 24 November 1903, a young man named George Robinson called at the Bank of England and asked to see the Governor. As Secretary, Kenneth Grahame went to see if he could help but was duly shot at. Luckily the bullet missed. A fire hose was used to overpower Robinson, who was later indicted for attempted murder but found to be of unsound mind. The incident left Kenneth unharmed but deeply shocked.

An Aspiring Author

Denied an academic career, Kenneth Grahame channelled his creativity into writing in his spare time. Being in London had its advantages. Here he became associated with literary circles, meeting leading writers of the day including Robert Browning, A.C. Swinburne and W.B. Yeats. He struck up a friendship with the charismatic Dr Frederick James Furnivall – editor of the *New English Dictionary*, founder of several literary societies and a keen oarsman. Encouraged by Furnivall, Kenneth became the Honorary Secretary of the *New Shakespeare Society* and began submitting essays to London magazines.

▲ Kenneth Grahame by Frederick Hollyer, *c.*1890–1900. Of his own work, Grahame said: 'In my tales about children, I have tried to show that their simple acceptance of the mood of wonderment, their readiness to welcome a perfect miracle at any hour of the day or night, is a thing more precious than any of the laboured acquisitions of adult mankind.'

BY ROYAL APPROVAL

Kaiser Wilhelm II, the last German Emperor and King of Prussia (reigned 1888–1918) had two books in the English language in the cabin of his royal yacht – the Bible and Kenneth Grahame's *The Golden Age*.

In 1888, *By a Northern Furrow*, which describes the Berkshire Downs in winter, was published in the *St James Gazette*. More essays – mostly about the countryside – appeared in other publications, including the *National Observer*. Its eccentric and influential editor, W.E. (Bill) Henley, welcomed Kenneth into his group of regular contributors. Kenneth even wrote for the radical magazine of the day, *The Yellow Book*.

Pagan Papers, a collection of essays, was published in 1893, followed by *The Golden Age*, stories about a group of children, in 1895. This book became a classic of its day and brought Kenneth literary acclaim. Succeeded by *Dream Days* in 1898, both books were successful in Britain and the USA, and are based on Kenneth's own experiences of Victorian childhood. Written for adults about childhood, the stories are presented from the perspective of a child reacting to the adult world around him. They demonstrate Kenneth's clear memory of what it felt like to be a boy. His close friend, artist and playwright W. Graham Robertson, said: 'Anyone who wants to know Kenneth Grahame may still find him in *The Golden Age* and *Dream Days*, the eternal boy, keenly alive to the beauty and wonder of the world around him, yet shy of giving expression to the strange happiness that bubbles up within him.'

Family Life:
Elspeth and Mouse

In 1897, Kenneth Grahame met Elspeth Thomson, daughter of the Scottish inventor Robert William Thomson. Also born in Edinburgh, she had moved to London with her widowed mother, who re-married; guests from the fields of art, science and literature were often welcomed into their home. Kenneth, considered a very eligible bachelor, was apprehensive of the opposite sex. The dreamy, romantic Elspeth, however, set her sights on him. They wrote to each other in 'baby-talk', using the nicknames Minkie and Dino. Despite reservations on both their parts, they married in July 1899 in Fowey, Cornwall, where Kenneth had been convalescing after a serious chest infection and operation. Sadly, on their return to London the marriage quickly became unhappy. Elspeth was not on Kenneth's intellectual level; while she pined for attention he preferred the uncomplicated company of his male friends, or time by himself.

In May 1900 their only child, Alastair (nicknamed 'Mouse'), was born. Wishing his son to experience the kind of happiness he himself had enjoyed as a boy in Berkshire, Kenneth moved the family back

➤ Elspeth and Kenneth Grahame (centre) with Elspeth's sister Winifred and brother Courtauld Thomson.

to his childhood dream-place, Cookham Dean, in 1906, where father and son enjoyed country walks. Kenneth wrote: 'I feel I should never be surprised to meet myself, as I was when a little chap of five, suddenly coming round a corner.'

Alastair's parents were regularly absent in his early years: Kenneth often stayed in London during the week; Elspeth went for prolonged stays at spas for her delicate health; the boy missed his parents deeply. Surrounded mostly by female house-staff, he could be precocious and wilful but was also creative and sociable. Encouraged by his governess, he produced several of his own little magazines called *The Merry Thought*, which included stories he had made up with contributions from family, visitors and neighbours.

◄ Born prematurely and blind in one eye, Mouse was doted on as a boy.

➤ Cookham Dean, where at first the Grahames rented The Hillyers and then Mayfield (now Herries Preparatory School).

Whispers on the Wind

Alastair loved books from an early age and his father delighted in reading him bedtime stories. By the time Alastair was four years old they had exhausted the supply of nursery storybooks and Kenneth turned to his own creative talents.

One May evening in 1904, waiting to go to a dinner engagement, Elspeth asked the maid impatiently, 'Where *is* Mr Grahame, Louise?'; she replied, 'He's with Master Mouse, Madam: he's telling him some ditty or other about a toad.' From then on, tales about Mr Toad and his friends developed in Kenneth's imagination and continued to be told to Alastair.

The stories became more defined in 1907 when Alastair was sent to Littlehampton, Sussex, with his governess while his parents holidayed in Cornwall. On 10 May Kenneth wrote his son a letter with birthday wishes and added as a postscript an episode about Toad. Over the next four months he wrote a further 14 letters from Cornwall and London, continuing Mr Toad's adventures. The governess, Miss Naomi Stott, had the foresight to save the early letters sent to Littlehampton and returned them to the Grahames. Together with later ones sent to Cookham Dean, they formed the basis of all the chapters about Toad in the book that was to come. Kenneth had not written anything since he married but, pressed by Alastair to put the bedtime stories into letter-form, he seems to have enjoyed the experience and perhaps carried on as much for himself as for his son.

Later, Elspeth liked to believe that she was the driving force behind Kenneth transforming the letters into a book. However, the main impetus came from Constance Smedley, European representative of the American magazine *Everybody's*. She lived at nearby Bray and, urged by her editor, visited the Grahames at Cookham Dean

▲ The first of 15 letters sent to Alastair by his father, which included stories of Toad.

◄ Mouse, whose love of bedtime stories spurred his father to start telling him tales about a toad.

to try and persuade Kenneth to write again, as many others had tried and failed to do.

Kenneth told Constance that he found writing a painful process. However, on overhearing Alastair's bedtime tales of Mr Toad she pointed out that a book was as good as written: the years of developing the characters and themes and the beautifully crafted letters need only be brought together. Kenneth agreed and, when not at the Bank, stayed at the London house to work on additional chapters and produce a final manuscript. By Christmas 1907 it was complete.

Inspirations and Settings

Ideas and themes for *The Wind in the Willows* had been forming in Kenneth Grahame's mind for many years. Childhood reminiscences clearly played a part and his magical time in Granny Ingles' garden was to leave a lasting impression of boyhood, reflected in his earlier essays.

The River

Many locations have laid claim to being the inspiration for places described in *The Wind in the Willows* and Kenneth evoked in his book a rich mix of settings that he had experienced and knew well. A river flows throughout the story and the Thames and its environs, especially in Berkshire and Oxfordshire, were clearly influential.

➤ 'Rounding a bend in the river, they came in sight of a handsome, dignified old house of mellowed red brick, with well-kept lawns reaching down to the water's edge.'

▼ Mapledurham House, near Reading.

The river at Fowey was also very significant. Kenneth Grahame had taken many holidays in the small Cornish town, where he had made some of his closest friends. Sir Arthur Quiller-Couch (known as 'Q') was a fellow author, who lent Kenneth his skiff to explore the local backwaters; Edward 'Atky' Atkinson was the eccentric Commodore of the Fowey Yacht Club; while Austin Purves was a visitor from America with whom Kenneth formed a close bond.

Toad Hall

Although many grand houses have been cited as the 'original' Toad Hall, Toad's riverside residence was probably a blend of several places

PRIVATE
NO LANDING
ALLOWED

MOLE ENCOUNTERS THE RIVER

'Never in his life had he seen a river before – this sleek, sinuous, full-bodied animal, chasing and chuckling, gripping things with a gurgle and leaving them with a laugh… All was a shake and a shiver – glints and gleams and sparkles, rustle and swirl, chatter and bubble. The mole was bewitched, entranced, fascinated.'

The Wind in the Willows

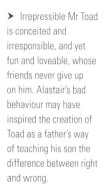
▲ The River Fowey, Cornwall. Kenneth's boating trip in 1907 from Fowey to Lerryn with friends Atky, Purves and his sons is said to have particularly inspired Mole and Ratty's picnic trip.

▲ Dr Frederick James Furnivall, out sculling on the Thames on his 85th birthday in 1910. 'Believe me, my young friend, there is nothing – absolutely nothing – half so much worth doing as simply messing about in boats.' (*The Wind in the Willows*)

that Kenneth knew of. The Fowey Hall Hotel maintains it was the inspiration, while a popular choice is Mapledurham House, near Reading, which is built from beautiful mellow brick. Other possibilities close to the Thames are Harleyford Manor, near Marlow, and the National Trust property Cliveden; although built of white stone, it is set above a wonderful stretch of the river. A convincing contender is Bisham Abbey, close to Cookham Dean. Built from red brick and stone, it even has a secret passage: 'There – is – an – underground – passage,' said the Badger impressively, 'that leads from the river bank, quite near here, right up into the middle of Toad Hall.'

➤ Quarry Wood, close to Cookham Dean, was the likely stimulus for the Wild Wood.

PANTHEISM

Kenneth Grahame found empathy with Pantheism, which had attracted interest in Victorian Britain. For him, Pan was god of meadows, forests, creatures and music, who lived in an idyllic and safe world. He appeared in some of Kenneth's earlier writings and came to the fore in *The Wind in the Willows*, in the chapter 'The Piper at the Gates of Dawn': '... whispered the Rat, as if in a trance. "Here, in this holy place, here if anywhere, surely we shall find him!"'

Characters

When developing his characters, Kenneth seemed to draw inspiration from several people close to him. Toad is thought to represent Alastair, a spoilt and headstrong child. Poetical, cultured and boat-loving Ratty combines aspects of Frederick James Furnivall, Edward Atkinson and Sir Arthur Quiller Couch, whilst Furnivall can also be seen in Pan.

There is a little of Kenneth himself in Ratty, too, who is enchanted by Pan and tempted by the possibility of escape. The author might also have seen himself in Badger, the kindly and conservative stalwart of decent behaviour, and in naïve, romantic Mole who discovers the wonders of the river and its friendly society.

➤ Irrepressible Mr Toad is conceited and irresponsible, and yet fun and loveable, whose friends never give up on him. Alastair's bad behaviour may have inspired the creation of Toad as a father's way of teaching his son the difference between right and wrong.

The Wind in the Willows

Although *The Wind in the Willows* is regarded as being written for children, it equally engages an adult audience. The story follows the adventures of a group of animal friends, who speak and act as humans. They live in an idyllic English countryside, enjoying the pleasures of life, free from the dangers of the Wide World beyond, while overcoming the terrors of the Wild Wood, and finally banishing the threat of invasion.

Mr Toad's adventures form the main story. Toad squanders his inheritance on the temptations of the modern age, behaves disgracefully, lets his friends down and neglects the responsibilities of his status, which puts the river-bankers' way of life in jeopardy – saved only by the efforts of his loyal friends.

Below the surface, the story provided Kenneth Grahame with a form of escapism from the pressures of adulthood. It celebrates companionship, loyalty and integrity and symbolizes the passing of an old world, steeped in traditional values, and the coming of a new and disagreeable one. The main characters are all men, perhaps reflecting Kenneth being more comfortable in the presence of his male friends.

▲ Toad becomes hopelessly addicted to motor cars – part of an increasingly industrialized world that Kenneth deplored: 'The *real* way to travel! The *only* way to travel! Here to-day – in next week to-morrow! Villages skipped, towns and cities jumped – always somebody else's horizon! O bliss! O poop-poop! O my! O my!'

Grahame was a great wordsmith and his poetic prose displays empathy and remarkable powers of description. Since much of the story evolved through speaking it out loud, the sounds of the words are almost musical; this lyrical style is captivating, holding the reader spellbound. His deep love of nature and affinity with animals makes the characters believable and endearing.

◀ The river-bankers (including Rat, Mole and Badger) represent a genteel way of life, while the marauding wild-wooders (stoats and weasels) stand for a hostile, common way of life, which threatens the rural idyll.

THE HONESTY OF NATURE

'As for animals, I wrote about the most familiar and domestic in *The Wind in the Willows* because I felt a duty to them as a friend. Every animal, by instinct, lives according to his nature. No animal, in other words, knows how to tell a lie. Every animal is honest. Every animal is straightforward. Every animal is true – and is, therefore, according to his nature, both beautiful and good. I like most of my friends among the animals more than I like most of my friends among mankind.'

Kenneth Grahame

Getting Published

After the manuscript was finished, it was to be ten months before the book was published. Although editors had long awaited another Kenneth Grahame book, they reportedly found his story about an animal world too fantastical and could not foresee its popularity. The Americans refused it and Bodley Head turned it down flat. At last Methuen & Co agreed to take it on but, being sceptical, refused any advance royalties.

The company had been founded in 1889 by Sir Algernon Methuen Marshall Methuen (formerly Stedman) to publish text books and educational works. Gradually the firm extended to other books, and after successfully bringing out *Barrack-Room Ballads* and further poetry by Rudyard Kipling it diversified into novels and children's literature. *The Wind in the Willows* and the works of A.A Milne were the most significant of these published during the early 1900s.

The original title proposed was *The Wind in the Reeds*, but this was too close to a book of poems by W.B. Yeats called *The Wind Among the Reeds*. Kenneth's second choice was *Mr Mole and His Mates*, while his friend W. Graham Robertson put forward *The Lapping of the Stream, The Whispering Reeds, River Folk* and *The Children of Pan*. Finally, *The Wind in the Willows* was agreed upon. To announce the book Kenneth was asked to write a piece for the publisher's catalogue: 'It is a book of Youth, and so perhaps chiefly for youth, and those who still keep the spirit of youth alive in them: of life, sunshine, running water, woodlands, dusty roads, winter firesides; free of problems, clear of the clash of sex; of life as it might fairly be supposed to be regarded by some of the small things, "That glide in grasses and rubble of woody wreck".'

The Wind in the Willows was finally published in October 1908.

◀ First page of Kenneth Grahame's completed manuscript.

◀ Front cover of the first edition in 1908, depicting Pan, Mole and Ratty. About his writing the author said, 'Writing is not easy … There is always a pleasure in that exercise; but, also, there is always an agony in the endeavour … It is, at best, a pleasurable agony.'

First Responses

Following its publication, *The Wind in the Willows* met a stunned silence and hesitant sales. By no means an immediate success, it seemed readers who had so admired Kenneth Grahame's earlier work could not accept his new venture into writing primarily for, rather than about, children. A review in *The Times* read: 'Grown-up readers will find it monstrous and elusive, children will hope, in vain, for more fun. Beneath the allegory ordinary life is depicted more or less closely, but certainly not very amusingly or searchingly … For ourselves, we lay *The Wind in the Willows* reverently aside and again, for the hundredth time, take up *The Golden Age*.'

However, its magic finally began to enchant readers. The American President, Theodore Roosevelt, already a fan of *The Golden Age* and *Dream Days*, wrote in January 1909: 'My dear Mr Grahame … at first I could not reconcile myself to … accept the toad, the mole, the water-rat and the badger … But after a while Mrs Roosevelt and two of the boys, Kermit and Ted, all quite independently, got hold of *The Wind Among the Willows* and took such delight in it that I began

▲ Badger, Toad, Ratty and Mole, the four main characters in *The Wind in the Willows*.

to feel that I might have to revise my judgment … Now I have read it and reread it, and have come to accept the characters as old friends; and I am almost more fond of it than your previous books.'

The Hon. Alfred Deakin, then Prime Minister of Australia, described the book as 'a prose poem perfect within its scope, style and sentiment, and rising to a climax in the vision of Pan – a piece of imaginative insight, to which it would be hard to find a parallel anywhere'.

MILNE'S WARNING

A.A. Milne, author of the Winnie-the-Pooh books, said: 'One does not argue about *The Wind in the Willows* … The book is a test of character. We can't criticize it, because it is criticizing us. But I must give you one word of warning. When you sit down to it, don't be so ridiculous as to suppose that you are sitting in judgement on my taste, or on the art of Kenneth Grahame. You are merely sitting in judgement on yourself. You may be worthy: I don't know, but it is you who are on trial.'

◄ A. A. Milne and his son, Christopher Robin, photographed by Howard Coster in 1926.

Early Illustrators

No other English children's book has been illustrated by so many different artists – over 90 since 1908. To interpret and depict a story and its characters pictorially is a responsible undertaking. In the case of *The Wind in the Willows*, it is a particular challenge to capture the personalities of the anthropomorphised animals convincingly.

The first 1908 edition was unillustrated except for a frontispiece designed by W. Graham Robertson. A fellow Scot, artist and playwright Robertson had been the first person to read the story before its publication. He said: 'I well remember my joyful enthusiasm when I first read the manuscript … There was then some talk of my providing illustrations, but time was lacking and, moreover, I mistrusted my powers, for I could not number an otter or a water-rat among my

➤ W. Graham Robertson's illustration showing three babies and an otter by a waterfall: the frontispiece of the first edition, 1908.

acquaintances though I had once known a mole almost intimately and had several toad friends ….'

Fully illustrated editions followed, the work of American artists Paul Bransom (1913, Charles Scribner's Sons), Nancy Barnhart (1922, Charles Scribner's Sons) and British artist Wyndham Payne (1927, Methuen & Co) – but never to Kenneth's satisfaction: 'My animals are not puppets; they always make them puppets.'

In 1930 Ernest H. Shepard was invited by Methuen & Co to produce drawings for a new edition. Already well known for illustrating *Winnie the Pooh* and other A. A. Milne books, he had also worked on *The Golden Age* and *Dream Days*, but was apprehensive about *The Wind in the Willows*: 'When I was commissioned to illustrate *The Wind in the Willows* in 1930, I hesitated, as I considered it so perfect a work of art in itself that no pictures could do justice to it, but I learnt that it had been illustrated already by various artists, none of whom, to my mind, had made a success of it. I suppose I felt that I could do better than this, anyway, I could try.'

◀ Illustration by Paul Bransom, first published by Charles Scribner's Sons in 1913, in the USA.

▼ E.H. Shepard in 1932.

Ernest H. Shepard

Ernest Howard Shepard (1879–1976) was born in London to an artistic and musical family. As a child he showed extraordinary artistic skill and, after attending St Paul's School, was encouraged by his father to go to art college. Earning two scholarships he entered the Royal Academy Schools as one of its youngest students. During the First World War he rose to the rank of major and was awarded the Military Cross for bravery in the field. He had regularly sent drawings to *Punch* during the war years and later was invited to join the 'table' (editorial team) of the magazine. Here he met E.V. Lucas, who was Chairman of Methuen at the time and introduced Shepard to A. A. Milne.

➤ Kenneth Grahame told Ernest Shepard: 'I love these little people, be kind to them.'

◀ Shepard first produced some colour illustrations for a 1959 publication of *The Wind in the Willows*, and added colour to his original illustrations ten years later.

▲ Other characters in the story include the Otter: 'They found themselves standing on very edge of the Wild Wood … The Otter, as knowing all the paths, took charge of the party ….'

SHEPARD'S VIEW

'I was lucky to have an introduction to Kenneth Grahame given me by a friend and armed with this I went over to his house at Pangbourne on the Thames, he was very kind but I think he rather feared another illustrator! He told me of the spots on the river where his little animals lived and where to find them all, where was Toad Hall, where Rat kept his little boat. He said he himself would take me to these places but he was too infirm.

Armed with his instructions and my sketch book I set out. It was very peaceful in the meadows by the river and I kept as quiet as possible as I moved along the bank – some movement in the grass might perhaps mean that mole was about or the line of bubbles on the water told me that rat was not far away. I looked for the tiny boat among the rushes and peered into the dark hole in the bank, fancying that I could see a pair of tiny eyes watching me. I stayed and sketched till the light failed, then I picked my way carefully across the fields, back to reality.

I was to see Kenneth Grahame once again. When I had made some drawings for the book I took them to Pangbourne. He was critical but I think he was pleased with my efforts and when he handed the drawings back to me he said, "I'm glad you've made them real." I always regret that he did not live long enough to see the new edition completed.'

E.H. Shepard, on illustrating *The Wind in the Willows*

▲ Toad, on the steps of Toad Hall, is confronted by his three friends.

Shepard proved the perfect illustrator, always sensitive to the mood of the text and placing the characters in settings that captured a sense of their surroundings. The resulting black and white illustrations completed in 1931 are lively, evocative and brimming with personality. Shepard's ready sense of humour and wit shine through, giving the characters human qualities whilst retaining their inherent animal natures.

During 1958 he undertook to produce eight coloured plates for a new edition of the book, followed by some further revised drawings in 1963 and culminating in 1969 in a full-colour version, published by Methuen & Co.

▲ Our heroes regain control of Toad Hall: 'There were but four in all, but to the panic-stricken weasels the hall seemed full of monstrous animals, grey, black, brown and yellow, whooping and flourishing enormous cudgels ….'

Arthur Rackham

"SHOVE THAT UNDER YOUR FEET,"
HE OBSERVED TO THE MOLE, AS HE PASSED IT DOWN INTO THE BOAT

◄ Arthur Rackham's illustrations for *The Wind in the Willows* were first published by Methuen & Co in the USA, eight years after Kenneth Grahame's death.

Arthur Rackham (1867–1939) was a prolific and highly successful English painter and illustrator, active during the so-called 'Golden Age' of illustration, and popular in both Britain and the USA. He worked on lavishly produced gift books and children's literature, such as *Grimm's Fairy Tales*, *Alice's Adventures in Wonderland* and *A Midsummer Night's Dream*.

He was especially gifted at illustrating fairy tales where his exquisitely drawn fairies, witches and gnomes were both beautiful and grotesque in equal part. They often lived amongst anthropomorphised trees, whose human faces and limbs became a trademark feature of Rackham's work and heightened the fantastical settings of the scenes portrayed. His soft colours and detailed style evoked a sense of age and enchantment, and were particularly suited to the three-colour separation printing process of the time.

Kenneth Grahame had always thought Rackham would be the ideal illustrator for *The Wind in the Willows*, but the artist turned down an early offer to illustrate the book due to pressure of work, which he later regretted. When he finally accepted the commission in the late 1930s, Kenneth Grahame was long dead and it was to be the last book Rackham worked on. Rackham died shortly after completing the illustrations and never saw the work in print, which was first published posthumously in the USA in 1940 and then in Britain in 1951 – the 100th edition of the book.

IT WAS A GOLDEN AFTERNOON;
THE SMELL OF THE DUST THEY KICKED UP
WAS RICH AND SATISFYING

THE OPEN ROAD

'At last the horse was caught and harnessed, and they set off, all talking at once, each animal either trudging by the side of the cart or sitting on the shaft, as the humour took him. It was a golden afternoon. The smell of the dust they kicked up was rich and satisfying; out of thick orchards on either side of the road, birds called and whistled to them cheerily.'

The Wind in the Willows

Life after The Wind in the Willows

In 1910 the Grahames moved to Boham's Farmhouse in Blewbury, Oxfordshire, with the Berkshire Downs on their doorstep, where Kenneth enjoyed walking. It was at his Blewbury home that he entertained a visiting American professor, Clayton Hamilton, in 1910, and told him: 'I doubt very much if I shall ever write another book … The effort is enormous … To toil at making sentences means to sit indoors for many hours, cramped above a desk. Yet, out of doors, the wind may be singing through the willows ….'

Alastair Grahame, meantime, had never settled at school, lasting only two weeks at Rugby and two terms at Eton. Home tutoring was more successful but unhappiness prevailed again at university. Accepted at Christ Church, Oxford, due to his father's influence, he struggled with the work and high expectations. On 8 May 1920, during his second year, he was found dead on the railway tracks in Port Meadow. Although doubts were raised, the inquest returned a verdict of accidental death, which Kenneth and Elspeth firmly clung to. However, it seems probable that it was suicide.

Devastated, Kenneth and Elspeth escaped to Italy, travelling around until 1924 when they returned and bought Church Cottage in Pangbourne, Berkshire. Between further trips to Italy, they lived a quiet and reclusive life here, enjoying their garden and proximity to the Thames. Kenneth finally took up his pen again

to write the foreword to George Sanger's circus memoirs, *Seventy Years a Showman*, in 1925 and some early recollections of schooldays in *Oxford Through a Boy's Eyes* in 1926. He refused, however, to write an autobiography.

Kenneth Grahame died on 6 July 1932, aged 73. At his funeral, the church of St James the Less, Pangbourne, was filled with flowers and cards from children, and with willows gathered from the river that morning. Although buried at Pangbourne, he was later transferred to Holywell Cemetery, Oxford, to lie beside his son.

◄ Alastair Grahame, photographed as an undergraduate at Oxford University.

▼ The epitaph on Kenneth's gravestone, written by his cousin Anthony Hope Hawkins (author of *The Prisoner of Zenda*): 'To the beautiful memory of Kenneth Grahame, husband of Elspeth and father of Alastair, who passed the River on 6th July 1932, leaving childhood and literature through him the more blest for all time.'

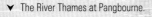

▼ The River Thames at Pangbourne.

Kenneth Grahame's Legacy

A fter Kenneth Grahame's death, many tributes were written which reflected his genius as an author, and the esteem in which he was held. In his 1933 book, *Frater Ave Atque Vale, A Personal Appreciation of the late Kenneth Graham,* Clayton Hamilton wrote: 'And yet it is a truth that, on that day, the translators of the King James version of the Bible, seated at an eternal council-table, admitted to their fellowship the last great master of English prose, and that Great Britain lost the loveliest of all her living souls.'

Films, plays and books

The Wind in the Willows remains one of the best loved of all children's books. Since 1908 it has never been out of print and by 1951 one hundred different editions had been published. It has been translated into several languages, been abridged, annotated

➤ A display in the River & Rowing Museum shop.

⋏ Kenneth Grahame by John Singer Sargent, 1912. In a letter to Elspeth Grahame, Constance Smedley wrote: '... he never seemed very interested in himself nor his writing but he was passionately interested in everything about riverlife and the outdoor world: in noble literature: in "all things lovely and of good report".'

TOAD OF TOAD HALL

A.A. Milne, famous for his children's verse and Winnie-the-Pooh books, began his literary career as a playwright. He loved *The Wind in the Willows* and introduced the book to the stage with his script *Toad of Toad Hall.* 'I have not made a play of *The Wind in the Willows.* But I have, I hope, made some sort of entertainment, with enough of Kenneth Grahame in it to appease his many admirers, and enough of me in it to justify my name upon the title-page,' he said. First performed at The Playhouse, Liverpool, on 1 December 1929, with incidental music by Harold Fraser-Simson, it was a triumph. Kenneth Grahame was thrilled that the book had been dramatized and invited Milne to share a box with him and Elspeth to watch a performance. The play continues to be performed and delight audiences around the world.

RATTY'S REFUGE

In 2009, at the River & Rowing Museum in Henley on Thames (see details on inside back cover), Alan Titchmarsh opened Ratty's Refuge – the UK's first garden designed to encourage water voles back to the banks of the Thames. The beautiful willow-edged garden aims to inspire and motivate gardeners to help conserve the water vole, and is used by the museum's education team with school groups. The Chelsea-medal-winning garden can be viewed from the museum's terrace.

▲ A water vole in its natural habitat.

▲ Ratty's Refuge.

◄ Member's badge from the River & Rowing Museum's Henley 100 Club.

and adapted for film, television and the theatre several times over, and plans continue for future stage and screen versions.

Sequels, short stories and counter-texts have all been motivated by Grahame's masterpiece, most notably William Horwood's *Tales of the Willows* and Jan Needle's *The Wild Wood*. In addition, clubs, societies and commercial merchandise have all taken inspiration from the iconic characters over the years.

Conservation of the water vole

Ratty, a main character in *The Wind in the Willows*, is, in fact, a water vole. At the time Kenneth Grahame was writing his story, water voles were widespread in Great Britain. However, the mammal has disappeared from 90 per cent of its former range since 1900, the result of loss of habitat caused by increased agriculture and predation from American mink, which were introduced to Britain in the 1920s for the fur industry but escaped or were released into the countryside.

The Berks, Bucks and Oxon Wildlife Trust, in partnership with the Environment Agency, British Waterways and Thames Water, launched the Water Vole Recovery Project in 1998, to arrest the decline across the three counties and to increase the water vole population. BBOWT is always keen to hear about sightings of water voles (see contact details on page 20).

Further Information

T he **River & Rowing Museum** in Henley is a major visitor attraction with links to *The Wind in the Willows* – see panel opposite. Listed below are details of a selection of other places with links to Kenneth Grahame and his famous story, though there are many others. Please contact the venues for opening times and admission charges.

The Bank of England Museum,
Bartholomew Lane, London EC2R 8AH
020 7601 5545
www.bankofengland.co.uk
The Bank of England Museum tells the story of the Bank of England from its foundation in 1694 to its role today as the United Kingdom's central bank, and includes material about Kenneth Grahame. This free museum includes permanent displays as well as changing exhibitions.

Bodleian Library, Broad Street, Oxford OX1 3BG
01865 277162
www.bodleian.ox.ac.uk
Kenneth Grahame bequeathed all the royalties in his works to 'the University of Oxford for the benefit of the Bodleian Library'. The collection holds the author's original manuscript of *The Wind in the Willows* and the 15 letters written to Alastair in 1907. See the online exhibition:
www.bodleian.ox.ac.uk/bodley/about/exhibitions/online/witw

Holywell Cemetery, St Cross Road, Oxford OX1 3UH
Picturesque Holywell Cemetery, in the heart of Oxford, is a haven for wildlife, and the final resting place of Kenneth and Alastair Grahame.

Cliveden, Taplow, Maidenhead, Berkshire SL6 0JA
01628 605069
www.nationaltrust.org.uk/cliveden
One of the possible inspirations for Toad Hall. Cliveden House is now a luxury hotel, set in magnificent gardens in the care of the National Trust. Guided tours of the gardens and house are available at certain times of the year. (For hotel bookings call 01628 668561; www.clivedenhouse.co.uk.)

Mapledurham Estate, Mapledurham, Reading, Berkshire RG4 7TR
0118 972 3350
www.mapledurham.co.uk
One of the possible inspirations for Toad Hall. The Mapledurham Estate is a venue for public events and private functions. Mapledurham House, its working watermill and St Margaret's Church on the estate can all be visited.

◀ The Bank of England Museum.

➤ The Bodleian Library.

Berkshire
Buckinghamshire
Oxfordshire

Berks, Bucks and Oxon Wildlife Trust www.bbowt.org.uk
As well as working to save the water vole (see page 19), the BBOWT runs wildlife campaigns, holds fun wildlife events and trains conservationists. It also has over 80 nature reserves where visitors can enjoy days out. BBOWT is always keen to hear about sightings of water voles: email watervole@bbowt.org.uk.

Furnivall Sculling Club www.furnivall.org
Founded by Dr F. J. Furnivall in 1896, this lively rowing club is based on the Thames at Hammersmith in west London. The club welcomes new members of any rowing ability.

Kenneth Grahame Society www.kennethgrahamesociety.net
Dedicated to all those who appreciate the works of the author, with regular newsletters and a variety of events for members.

Information correct at time of going to press.